Things OK with you?

Things OK
with you?

Vincent O'Sullivan

Victoria University of Wellington Press

Victoria University of Wellington Press
PO Box 600, Wellington
New Zealand
vup.wgtn.ac.nz

A catalogue record is available from the
National Library of New Zealand.

ISBN 9781776564132

Printed in Singapore by Markono Print Media Pte Ltd

Contents

For Helen

* * *

For Michael Jackson
Poet, scholar, dear friend

After Lucy Tinakori's famous party

I love it that poetry now so possesses the world
it is not possible to play 'pin the tail' at a children's
party without every child being the winner
wherever the tail's pinned. Space is guaranteed
compliant the way thumb's fumbling's inevitably
spot on. Every child comes home
happy, 'I won just as much as Jane did!'
There's as many winning donkeys as smiling
kiddies, what a happy thing to realise so early on!

Only one child slapped (oh, but lightly)
as mum hauls her back to the Humvee
taking her home. Holly, her name, the spoiled
child who refused to play, who shouted, 'I
know I *lost*, stop saying I won!', and twice
on the drive back saw donkeys in paddocks
and tails *exactly* where she knew they had to be,
and said – slapped for that as well – 'See? *Arse.*'

Scar

It is only, one says, only what one expects,
essential, as it might be called in another story,
in books on other shelves: a waiting

figure turning from the window, the frail
track down to the river, like, you might say,
like the childhood scar seen slightly across

her upper lip, thin as cotton, where the edge
of tin bit at her as she slipped. *Only
what one expects*, an aunt had said, meaning

blood and sharpness pay for what one does,
but *essential*, this long after, as she turns
with the white curtain drawn into one fist,

billowy as her hand unclenches, and the thread
across her lip defines her, defines us,
as I see it, a gift of great moment,

even now, with my step as hers on the timbered
floor, close enough for my finger to touch it,
time's almost invisible ridge: *like that, like that.*

What to look sets off

When the fireflies which you had never seen
come out in the evening you know where you're standing,
you know you are most certainly in a better place
than anywhere you might have in mind.

I say that because I thought that
on the smooth lawn outside a retirement village
in New Jersey, visiting the mother
of a woman I greatly cared for. Fireflies, as here,
may be a way of not needing to talk of love.

The metaphorically incontinent might have a field
day, let loose on the stir of fireflies
at a time you never expect them.
Yet *Look at me!* the fireflies remind you,
nothing is like us exactly so look again.
You are not walking among tiny express trains
nor coming close to clipped fairy enchantments
nor have reason to imagine should a thought slow
sufficiently to see it, you might say, 'I am watching
thinking in a mind more interesting than my own.'
'These are fireflies', the total statement.

To drive back to the city is a very
ordinary thing. Even to ride beneath rivers,
the Holland Tunnel not so special as you thought,
coming up to the million-tiered
lights where you need to be, is like
nothing more than the million lights it is,
as you thought on the lawn of the Home
in New Jersey. The pulsing luck of seeing both.
What to look sets off.

The unexpected man

I stand in the corner of a world
that is more curious than essential to me,
I look across a narrow slug of water,
watch a swayed cage clank tourists
over black surges to an island
where history behaved as history does,
badly. A town with my name above
shop doorways, across bar-room windows.
It is interesting more than moving.
Along the peninsula's gnawed edges
bright cottages play at local
colour, travellers stop for their serving
of accents, and under a tilted rock,
unexpected as annunciation, the Children
of Lir lie buried in time's perfected
down, myth's abiding stall.
Coins left by after-believers oxidise,
meld together, not a tribute
to swans so much as declaring,
I, I too have been here, I am part
of the story where the great wings lie.
The drive back across mountainy roads,
above curdling tides, in twilight passing
the one fact of the day still pure
fact: a naked man goes walking
ahead of the car, a mottling smear
on his shoulder, a man naked as fish.

Sentimental story

It is odd, this constant habit of ours
to adore the abandoned, the way children
from the richest bedrooms are quickened to tears
the shabbier the crib, the mangier the cattle
with consoling eyes, the shepherds the better
for their rags and itches, before the kings
in their cardboard crowns and mock brocades
bring us into the picture, we *gens fortunés*,
because the shepherds will smile at the kings
with their golden boxes, and the kings
at the white as white sheep at the foot of the crib:
we are sad together and exult together
and with luck the child will put things right,
this child who knows it is something very different,
the end of the story and the middle are very different,
and the classes marched out in step
from the institutions, their breaths stinking,
their piss-smell clothes, get the weirdest nod
from the cagey infant: *Let's bide our time.*

'Something not to be mentioned to Mrs Dooley'

Wallace Stevens

Which is so much, covered and uncovered.
Which is this and that tapping at the blind.
Which is rumour in the kitchen, fact at the fence.
Which is flying colours so nicely who doesn't salute?

Mrs Dooley who has seen it all, shocked over and over
so nothing surprises, next to nothing
delights. There is a white swan on the mantel
holds matches between its wings. A Russian doll

pregnant with armies – what else? – of dolls.
At Xmas trains tinnily hoot in and out of tunnels,
so tiny the nudge of a mouse brings a mountain down.

There's a man would give her a hand she'd certainly slap.
A God who doesn't go much on the world he's made.
A song called 'Here in a tick', by the Close to Heart.

Late note to Iris Murdoch

We read a poem, a story, that begins,
'a philosopher is sitting in a book-lined room',
our assumption the following sentences
will tell you, 'while a woman is threading

a needle in the kitchen', 'a boy is
rubbing a footy boot to a black lighthouse',
'an old man fingers his blanket, nice
as remembering skin'. The philosopher

has a window shaded against distraction,
as the needle is threaded, the boots
set brightly right, memories not always
regrets, which is good to know. The sky

arches the houses where such things occur,
the light rises, the dark returns, the game
is played and nearly won, the sewing
inches closer to what it intends, the young man

in the dream wakes to age as if that is the dream.
The philosopher has considered needles, soaring punts,
the bluish hand on the counterpane, a glass
out of reach. *Realismus* as he writes it.

He'd rather say it in English which isn't quite as good.
He'll think on it further, as the needle thinks
for the woman, the heft for the boy,
whatever is coming to mind, as the thinking ends.

Lines from way back

The senate seethes, as in an emperor's reign.
The deals are done, speeches endorse the corpse.
Pussy and circuses stake out their claim.
Immigrants, bankers, slip their varied hoops.
Maggots exult that nature bred them white,
their slither vermicules to get it Right.

He dreams the dream of being the nation's daddy.
He hands out presents, 'Souvenir the string.'
Zeus's scrotum carried by his caddy,
the perks of office hankering for his swing.
And a wink to bro Caligula, OK?
'All things trot for senators who neigh.'

Sentiment being a necklace you can wear when it's over

There's a man she likes to think of singing
'Over the Rainbow' as she sings it even
in her sloppy clothes, which she doesn't mind,
as he too is unconcerned about what the woman
wears or does not wear, as the words curve out
from his perspective:
                              Toto is the name
of a black dog with the knack of dashing
over the rainbow and back before the song
is ended, you can tell by the way
he pants, shifts from paw to paw, looks up
so buttons which a dog's eyes are often
said to look like, look like again:
                                        the man sings
and the girl sings and the dog's pretty much exhausted.
The rainbow hauls at its rope. That's how they meet.

As if the moon . . .

As if the moon so far as a poem goes gives a damn.
'God made me.' 'God didn't make me.' The moon
is the answer, whatever the question. Most things are.
The rabbi reads from his text, its pages flaring
so much holy moon. The non-believer brakes
beside the dazzled lake, stops to take it in,
feels his pulse pounding at so much more than 'moon'.
The sky bellows, that's how silent silence is.
Bleeds pure moon.

Riverrun

'You've scarcely seen me at it,' a modest river might
tell you, as if your presence is beside the point.

'The moment I'm under my first bridge it's a different
story, I comprehend distance as code

for current, the first kids leaning at a rickety
jetty hollering "Black!" as eights

blaze downstream.' Or, 'I am out of your depth,
even before we've passed.' Clocks squabble

diversely, taking the measure of rivers.
That placid stretch mirroring bronze poplars

ten minutes from Tamahere an hour later
warps to clawing wind, carries purple thunder.

The dim voice of a river ventriloquizes sky.
Look up. Stay down. How flung lace froths

the knees of the Falls. We know you deeply,
says a leaping lover. Beyond grasp, as it swirls.

Epistemology, Standard Five

'How we exist so differently,' Sister Gabriel said.
'Being', as it was explained, so the boy thought it,
not unlike the piled woodchips in the yard at the mill,
the mound of them, and us lined up for our scoop,
God as we thought the foreman tipping our share
into our lugged sacks, 'Being enough for you.'

Then Jeez, the sheer unfairness coming home!
'Being' was a swizz *per se* with its chancy extras!
His cousin Julia's legs. His brother's brains,
defective vision in his case so he had to squint
just to see how lovely she hurdled on Sports Day,
how his brother looked at the board, knew what to write.

'God wants you *to be*.' As if that's the whole story!
Wants you smiling so people love you. Wants you
to think, 'I have diverse gifts, just another kind,'
if coming home you're the runt even in the Reserves.
'But you equally hold the flag,' the scout master instructs,
'when you sing the words no one owns them more than you.'

So you play with a partner who says, 'Not just your
fault, mate.' Your high-fiving the champ, makes you
faster, does it? A bitter poem this, and rightly.
There is no going back to the mill there in stanza one.
Being clangs its door. No second queue.
'Get a load of this,' Being says, 'Make do, make do.'

Argentinian reprise

In defence of mock executions, the unassailable fact
that after the first, the real thing cannot be worse

than the squad's getting their eye in, than hearing
the click of finally living it through, the thud,

not again! It is knowing that bastard of
an officer who winked the first and second times,

will come at it again. 'The heart is never sated,'
he is telling you that, 'I can come at this, time

and again, which is more than you might.'
The man in the book which was not a novel

said he walked back to the cell, his heart too loud
to catch what a cellmate told him, the taste of coffee,

the curled lip of the cup he drank from, less
special than you might have thought had someone told

him, 'The coffee is always fresh, there's sausage on a plate.'
Whether this is the story of humanity, or something

worse, is a question he believes irrelevant as snow
powdering his shoulders. Going out. Marched back.

Captain Jackson's sonnet

One of my looming in-laws – a forebear of my wife –
goes butchering whales, drinks with Te Rauparaha, quotes
scripture to parsons, to terrified lads in his boats,
raising Leviathan's hulk at the ends of the earth

since a boy upped sticks from Putney years before the Treaty,
relying on God, his twenty-stone bulk, his bloody eye
when it came to razoring a lance, to letting it fly
so the depths rolled reddening the tides from Te-awa-iti

down the coasts of Te Pounamu and by Christ back,
violating language, out-mouthing Falstaff,
Job's nemesis flickering ahead like a tadpole in a dish.

That was Captain Jackson for you, ruling current and tack,
solid as Aoraki as he swivels his gaff,
master of all but his missus Eliza, who played Jimmy like a fish.

If you don't have a dog yourself well you'd hardly know

how the dog that walked on the beach and the lady
usually there behind it like to think it theirs, the beach,
the way the girl as well believing it's hers the most:
a thought that surprises as it first occurs: two people
        and a dog go walking three different beaches.

Dad telling her once dogs hear the tock of a heart
underneath what's there when the ground shakes cities
loose: likes to think for herself how a dog
maybe looks through waves as well as if through glass,
        so that's a stingray, that a shark?

No, not that exactly her father says,
but she loves it knowing how dogs so easily
know about *beneath* us, their scrabbly sniffing
at things as well higher up, so much further out,
        like hearing elastic snap way off.

So much that's nice there surely the way earthquakes
pack, broken old lines for us but so
skeined for a dog, its threading to how things lie
instead of just fussed, as we are, guessing,
        guessing at best. Lucky lady's dog.

Soon enough, then

The willows' cages trace the curving river.
Behind them, skeletal birches tell you,
'This is the story, the one you stand in.'

Snow loads the southern slopes.
Stones chucked from the wooden bridge bounce
on the river. A dropped mitten lies on ice.

A steer's breath smokes like a hearth.
A crack shocks, a distant gunshot.
The melt grinds, upstream.

By Friday the ice will nudge in chunks.
The one star you name drills above the range.
So little any longer certain. White too, something else.

Confessional verse

She is a woman he was once in love with
when he wrote bad verse that told her,
'her nipples are like tents in a desert.'

'As if you'd know,' she belittled him.
It was as if a coop of Hitchcock's birds
were flung across the kitchen.

He seemed to lose interest after that.
Poetry surely is more than pecking feathers?

Late shift

They have been so raucous, dreams, I cannot
believe it, how they come from nowhere.

The nowhere they step from is bigger,
meaner, than purgatory ever was,
as I tried to imagine it as a boy,
a place no one wanted to be, no wonder
we said novenas to prise them out.

In one, some of my best dead friends
turned out to see me executed. I was
more touched by that than apprehensive.

Sexual dwarves and silently vicious
children followed until I escaped.
But there they were, grinning, frisky,
their fingers crooked like a teacher's
calling you out to be caned.

Others malevolently reflected, faces
distant enough to entice, close enough
to repel. For minutes on waking I'd lie,
wishing my mind was someone else's.
And how worse the *nowhere*, if not mine?

'Don't give credence to Vienna,' a voice
instructs. Another, how thinking of dying's
a mild comfort, such dreams on prowl.
So that is what life was like, in different
colours? A way to make it nicer, is it,
waking from that? The slatted blinds
tilt sunlight, polished knives.

Rose-talk

Beneath Brunner roses in what the gardeners
call 'The Bower' visitors are encouraged to sit,
to enjoy nature deeply and think profoundly.

We know too much to be forgiven.
We forgive too much to be quite sincere.
We touch hands in the fabulous umbrage.

Most things we say tend to sound
as if meant to be chipped in marble,
which is simply the way shadows lie, about now.

A book we lend among ourselves tells us
how this profusion of loose roses,
introduced by Cecile Brunner,

has delighted ever since, grow
to four feet in theory, sometimes out of reach:
'Their glory is manifest until early frost.'

Only connect . . .

A man is watching the sea.
His line tremors, the man becomes
the sea. The blue that enlisted
forever, the uncounted sunsets,
the lines slanted like nylon rain
of those who fish close beside him,
waiting the sea to signal pain.
His arm jolts at the shock.
'A place to begin,' the reel sings,
'we are racked together.'

The story of Born Again Brightly, being the name I chose

I was in the waiting room
of the famous specialist
when my name was called,
not my name exactly,
but a nurse announcing matter-
of-factly, 'Will the man
with a million-dollar driveway,
a second Filipino spouse,
a biography half-commissioned,
a mantelpiece of silver trophies
for middle-distance hurdling,
speak with Dr Lopez now.'

The famous doctor nodded curtly.
He said, 'The soul too has its
cry for cosmetics,' this first
morning intent on removing
the desire for 'first among equals',
at which point I take in
the signed photographs of dictators
saluting his walls. On subsequent
mornings across several weeks
Dr Lopez operating deftly
on the smaller lesions of wealth,
on investment melanoma,
on impacted properties, ingrown
shares, devalued tumour.

He held aloft in forceps
the still palpitating nodule
of the soul's deep fascination
with itself, the memories

of women which may, as he said,
appear calcified yet nerves
will still respond, the various
ganglia of hardened envy,
and in the last and toughest
week, the dilated diaphragm
of ambition, its dates indicated
by striations as in rings on trees.

These procedures so variously
catalogued as *Spiritual Exercises*,
as *The Enlightened Way*, as *Nirvana
in Stitches rather than Tears*,
still others described in languages
that elude me, which the charge nurse
checks with a pencil as if no more
than a teacher ticking names
on sports days, ensuring the same
number of pupils exit the baths
as arrived by bus. She then briskly
assures all surgical removals
are disposed of according to
protocols of best practice.

There can only be room for
improvement. There is no going
back, you accept, once incisions
have been made, the transplants
themselves at a date to be decided
by further consultation with Dr Lopez
and his team. The nurse smiles for
the first time, *sororal*, the word.
Calls me graciously, Born Again Brightly,
as I am from now on in.

While it all goes on

this talk about awful things – 'You've scarce seen the bristle
of its snout, heard the scrape of its tampering
paw, caught its feculent whiff' –

so the preacher you've never heard but page-thumps in
old novels, as the master of taws in a grandfather's
story, *Just listen here* –

'God has them on file,' says the rheumy stranger
at a table at *Forget-me-not* in real life
South Dunedin,

'I know damn all but know that.' He sucks
at a cheese roll, he had asked, 'I'll have that beauty,'
tapping the cabinet,

and so sits with it now – as we spell it, 'a moment
of prey'. His finger dabs its perfection. God
comfy as a mouthful.

Floated in from the Heads, a slopped dead penguin
makes a schoolgirl think of a hand gone slack
inside a glove.

Bad said so often it spatters as if next thing
it's rain. Yet 'Snow this morning at Portobello' –
how's that for good?

Or 'Moonlight all over a carpark's still pretty
good moonlight.' Not the cheese-man insisting
that mind but a lady

with a hat sets old family photos breathing,
thinking it over in her corner. 'Very timely,' as she says
of Lipton's in its lovely cup.

Such a busy day

says the emperor, having thought it through,
'Before anything else, such is Fate, and last of all.'
There's a choice of nets, of tridents, knives of variously
adequate edges, chunks of lead should knuckles
be your chosen thing. And always the hesitant digit
so testing the blade strop, as the Imperator too,
hands sluggish in his lap, twirling the boredom
of *Can't we begin, for gods' sake*, his own thumb
mouse-nervy as to Up or Down, as the slobbed
mob yabbers? As the tiny eye through the helmet
presumes to hope? Sand, as he thinks at bedtime,
flipping Lucretius. Sand takes any colour.

Suburban variations

'Let's play at God,' the naughtiest child said,
his older sister amused, the younger brother
asking, 'Isn't that rude?'
                              Amusing and rude,
the naughtiest child tells him, Come on,
before we're caught.
                              Pretends to remove his sister's
rib, demanding, 'Don't you even know for God's sake
where we come from?';
                              advising his sibling, 'If you're
not inclined to kill me, how do we know we're
brothers?'
                    With their parents out at their
'Power to the People' meeting on local drainage,
the child goes into the room of illegal hydroponics,
snippers the choicest plants at the very roots.
                                        'There's
no story,' the boy announces, 'you can't tell like it's new.'
And 'By Christ,' as his Dad shouted coming back later,
'if we hadn't spoiled you rotten you'd have some
respect!'
                While his sister, slyly diverted, asking,
'Driven are we, Father, out of the garden?',
and the boy with the marks of cane considers
whatever the fabric of the heavens, the swirlings
of time, life tomorrow will be different.
                                        As God threatened all along.

How to shame a family properly, we vestigial Europeans

'So what's it like?' my mokopuna asks me,
'to be like, like really old?' So I say,
'Well, a bit like this, like going for a walk
when you probably should be somewhere else
and saying, "I don't mind telling this over again"',
and start listing this and that he can't comprehend –
the Eiffel Tower for one or the wobbly pillars
rather fancied in St Peter's, or a tiny beach
on Naxos where an old statue still lies that lay
not so much dog-tired as without the ordinary
luck ever to stand, as we do; or the grave (this
the harder one to explain to a child), the grave
of a darling man in Dublin who so loved Harry,
Dick and Tom, just that the rest, the *lot*,
he couldn't abide.
                    'Heavy stuff,' the boy's mother
says, a touch put out, 'for a simple question.'
She'd have liked me to come on, well, more tūrangawaewaed,
a good-natured codger humming along with Thomas Bracken.
But given the chance, I tell her, I'd like to be remembered
more as a man with a lobster on a coloured ribbon
people may be kind enough to pass off as a loon.

Once

Once in my life I've been fishing. A brother-
in-law assured, 'You don't need to talk out there,'

so we didn't. After an hour or so he lifted
this reluctant silvery strip

from its hook and walloped its head against
the ridge of the dinghy we sat in for those

aeons of hours off Rat Island, as some
people called it, this acre or so

of shallow crumbling yellowy cliffs
off the Herne Bay coast. That was fishing for me.

Oh, and another larger fish with scales
a bit like threshing diamonds racked

in the cradle of the dinghy until its life
went *phut*, a wet doused candle.

But until it did its heart I suppose was
tossed about in rage at air dreadful

as water might be for us. Until 'fishing'
stopped and it may as well have been a sock.

On the level

An admirable thing about Zola is when
he wrote *la table* he meant it,
completely. Table, where one's *grand-père*
and the one before him may have been
laid out, where weddings, christenings,
slopped local wines, farts the order of the day,
where a servant girl bore children,
the fathers buckling quickly – Christ,
a kitchen table's no Antoinette's chamber
but serves its turn, *eh bien*? How can you not
love Zola?
            Did Henry James so much
as guess what lay beneath the linen,
beneath 'covers for twelve' as they used
to say, once you hit the boards?
I stroke a two-hundred-year-old surface
in the café where I sit. I imagine
the young waiter on solitary drinkers –
the kicks they get from just sitting.
But ah! Zola's table.

Life writing

In a museum in Bordeaux I saw
Josephine Baker's Montmartre costume
of bananas and little else.
                                    The same museum
has a Roman mosaic that if you imagine
water freshly mopped across it must have been
among the loveliest things you'd seen.

And another exhibit a crude enough
plaster guess at Neanderthal forefolk
with their simple necklaces worn so proudly,
before we did for them, properly.

That was the same afternoon I almost
knocked a cyclist beneath a tram,
the utter carelessness of not attending.

Any wonder, if it's telling emblems
we're into, the Bordeaux museum and environs
put fairly neatly a sizeable chunk of my life.

In defence of the adjectival

An epithet you cannot get rid of
becomes, shall we say, a little house you abide in,
so when the clock dings, or the bird gargles,
the world knows he'll attend here any second,
the man who lives in the Swiss-chalet house.

Or you may think, 'What kind of mantis,
I ask you, if I don't say "praying"?'
A disappointed mantis I can tell you that.

Stripped of adjectives I've sometimes thought,
and you're Adam & Eve sauntering the Garden,
no one else in sight, as yet quite undecided
as to grasping at figleaves.

I know there are writing instructors
who'll tell you, 'Shy clear of the adjectival,'
as though they're telling hikers to avoid
tracks buzzed with wild honey.

What sort of instructor would tell you that?
One who fears the approaching drone.
Who hears the wing-chirrs of intent.
The little hive arriving for him to crouch to.

For the Time, Being

Hannah walks down from the mountains,
from the too conceivable lie of the brilliant mentor
tucked up against ice in his *schmaltzy* hut,
his wife Elfride diligent with strudel,
the locals proud of their man still dressed
as a souvenir.
        Blut, no doubt, should
he snick his finger, *Lebensraum* for the pitch
of the heightened mind.

        And the glorious girl
still attentive, half a lifetime later,
to the man who lauds how poetry springs
as thought demands it, *Dasein's*
proving beat. And what does she
think of as she leaves him?
        Unsurprising, it's love
we may say for mere fact as it is,
for the randomness of reality's sloping
back to valley floors,
        for plurality flung as an arc
plumes braking skis.

        Now back
from the track between the mountains, to the tiny
people as seen from the Master's window,
the size of oneself on whatever road –
        one
by one, she might count them. A million
for a start. A million then two and so on.
Counted in one's native tongue, it has to be

that. We count as we've learnt to count,
or it doesn't count.

The Jewish writer and philosopher Hannah Arendt visited Martin Heidegger, her former teacher, lover, Nazi, and author of Time and Being, *after the War.*

Whatever Japanese is for *Doppelgänger*

'Yuri went to the bank in Shimonoseki.'
A simple line in a letter stands solid as a lifetime.
I know nothing of Yuri nor the bank, little enough
of a prefecture of however many millions,
yet street after street, city beyond city,
where banks have been visited by innumerable Yuris.
There may even be one this minute who reads
a line in a letter about someone he will never
know, 'V.', say, 'who went to a Westpac
in South Dunedin.' There are five at least
people he spoke with during the morning.
The new chiropodist sign raises feet
to things of glamour. The Charity Centre
overflows. The closed Railway Workshops
indict a political party with the humanity
of stale lard. While Yuri who has never been here
may think of imaginary ice cliffs behind
South Dunedin, or tracts of desert, or supposes
we live in the spray of whatever Māori
may be for Niagara. I do as much for his city
should I try a little to raise, to resurrect it,
from the strung-out islands in the one old
atlas I have, 'The Empire of Japan' as it shows
you, which is not the way to say it any longer.
This morning he too has been to all sorts of places,
streets I cannot pronounce the names for, a bank
with a smiling teller, a severe assistant
whose thumb is slightly coloured from counting
bank notes with an accuracy we so depend on.
Yuri chatting of foreign places as he watches and waits.
Yuri who went to the bank in Shimonoseki.

The body off Lesbos

'How lovely and lonely and given to heroic choice,'
so we'd like to tell her, so she'd like to hear,
yet 'like' so seldom being as we like it
this is the day we share as if imagined,
the listing boat, the arrived at beach,
the wreck and the random of never reached,
the sea as the nature of sea intends:
the trivially filmed surf where pity ends.

End game

A lifelong but not nasty liar
to her dead but still lied-to spouse,
knitting her grandchildren cardies,
furrows complacent brows,

thinking the cosiest thoughts
in a kindly-as-ever world,
sharing a dab of arrowroot biscuit
with the white cat curled

in heraldic languor in its slab
of sun; as it stirs
it may seem an easy conscience
is a creature of abundant furs,

for how tiny deceits, grained singly,
build the Mountain of One-by-One,
as the cat craftily ripples
towards a nicer slice of sun,

as the moralist who watches
and presumes to condescend,
imagines a room without cats or kindness
from beginning to end.

Sacred texts

Truth as we lavishly tell it being the flag
to begin with, the closed fist holding the flag,
the script on the breeze's whicker destined
to instil:
        we prefer to see knees accept it,
the mind in its sweating foxhole of devout
concern.
        We stand on a hill observing
its dark demand, the outflanked flanks,
the bogging of columns, tactics' placid drone,
the gorgeous splintering hydrangeas wrenching half
the sky.
        All so there to behold. A boy fastens
a belt that unclasps him to glory, his eye
reflecting the flag in its millisecond's
rent,
        the instantly flung horizon
slick as God's intent. A detached arm
commas briefly against faultless sky.

The spook at life writing

I dislike biography – one's own, that is –
fairly much as I imagine the beans my wife's
planted in the garden behind the shed
would be the first to acknowledge the bamboo
pole is what guides them through to Xmas,
but even so, bugger that – to curl or
sprawl as one's disposed to by the scumble
of genes on the make, rather
than the straight and narrow we each tend
to become – that's what I'm inclined to.
The very word 'benign' will tell you someone's
sorting you out, you hear the chopped
fragments falling in the enamel pot, you
know you're there to be ladled to those
who watch the clock, demand to be
served. The bamboos of decorum
stake you from the start. So soon as you're
named, that's the first distortion,
you no longer so much as imagine what might
have become, the dark pulse attended,
our lost brotherly selves, the hidden code.
A fire before harvest's not a bad idea.

What *river* means

Never mind as old as she is or whenever, it's
how she remembers, a girl and watching
from the farm window with its copper beech,
back then when she so liked it the way the river
lifted its grey scrap from the lounge window,
a glinting stretch down at the iron bridge,
'the eelstrip' it's called just round the next curving
making her think how it's always wanting,
the river, to be the river miles ahead, like a sister
waiting to be her older sister:
                                    as the river
at Leamington's already the brightly slant of
so downstream, so exactly here as there,
the current's sickled swerve at Taupiri,
how she so liked that, the girl, to think of,
the sky's late inking the whole of the river
up to where the next bend's into bends ahead,
'till it reaches the Heads' so she hears and her watching,
puzzling, the beech's scraggle in the frailed light
across whatever scrap of moon's on hand;
as she'd like to say it but doesn't *the river so always*
tomorrow, any second ever yet always here,
right here at a thousand places, what river means.

Ms Dickinson, Mr Whitman

She may have heard how huge he was
how broad his pavements flowed,
the bandages on every branch
when civil tempests swerved –

as he perhaps would scarcely note
through neat domestic glass
the drilled battalions of the soul
patient embroidery knows –

the battlegrounds a sleeve can blur,
the snipering of a leaf,
the wheelings of an army's push
on needle-points of grief,

how those who lie in different camps
on different dyings watch –
and flare fraternal signals through
at midnight's gasping crush.

In Amherst, on the Potomac,
on shelves such aeons house –
the halt of currents on reserve
when silence breaks surprise.

Spot on

The rigmarole of to get there,
to things as they are.

The horde of 'begats' in the Bible
leading up to 'Voila!'

The amount of dark required
to say 'morning star'.

Lines for the iceboxes of High Baroque
for Dunstan

This is where *World* so dwindles to a jewel in space,
a diadem's rim against dark, dark's metallic sheen
as an astronaut takes it in, voice crackling earthwards:
'Major Tom to Bernini, *santissima* on screen.'

Signify

World, sometimes I doubt you. Even
that chair, say. The chair with the blue
canvas back of the kind you see with 'Director'
printed across it where movies are made.
The chair couldn't be more simple. I've placed
it there as a test, to check it exists next
morning. It is part of the nature of things
not to be depended on too deeply. Thus one
thinks about it: a cathedral with awesome
porticos, for example, balustrades' fat
forearms on important stairways, bells
at expected hours across aeons, thick
beating tongues: such iron faith
in the world, that's all I can say.
If it wasn't for *things* who'd believe in
more than things? Hence the moment I see
it, the blue canvas and the word 'Director'
on the back of the chair exactly as I left it,
well, you can say, what kind of a world
would you fancy, not to credit this?
As if there's a likely other you'd trust
to declare: the chair. The world it sits in.
The man whose being is to say so.
As is its, to survive.

Festival highlight

That dreadful urge a woman said
to write, there's so much to write,
but the words aren't there, you
know what it's like?, she asks
at a fiction workshop, the suffering
one goes through with that particular

version of distress? Embarrassment
hovers. The writer on stage nods kindly
as a nurse holding high a bottle
for transfusions as you sometimes
see in News from warzones.
She's crying, actually, the woman

who asked the question, a right
spectacle no one likes to say
outright, several writers
already shaping their forms of pity,
possible motives, stories on the make.
As the woman knows, which is why it hurts.

In praise of Gina the acrobat's deft daughter

It's a rare thing this day and age
to hear tributes such as this is, to expect
its persisting, yet I've heard not one
or two men use it, oh more than that,
and not friends only, but the occasional
person one speaks casually with as one does
and he says, not bitterly, but with undeniable
reverence, 'Never yet has she said goodbye,
not to one of us, yet.' And as others report:
'It was when we seemed so totally at home
one with the other, laughter no problem, nor
crying as something moved us deeply,
so we thought, "That's nice", that's surely how
people who love concur, and supposed
it was in her nature' – who wouldn't think that,
her family's profession through several
generations, as she'd deftly handstand on a bed
head, a chair back, a balcony's rim? Then
curl the air about her, that's one way to put
it, and unfold, a jack-knife; if your breath
hadn't billowed pure surprise already,
it fanned as she angled back, hair a streaming
curtain, a drench of blonde-bright rain
her leaning forward, eel-gifted swervings
into air-born grace: and as her heels planted
and you waited her arms raised in the kind of high
Voila! we're accustomed to wait for with those
supremely gifted in such performance – Gone!
Not one she said goodbye to, and the element
most of us thought might be ours as well
struck off, refashioned as vacant space.

The end of any account very much as this is –
not a word said, not a note inscribed, yet never
a person I've heard of – this the weirdly aspect –
who carries grudges, talks of damaged Troy.
See you then was never in it. Just *Not there* bestowed.

In foreign stories

I liked the man who walked through cities
much as he walked through his distant village,
knowing the difference was not big houses
or small houses but in the head of the man

who walked there knowing light was the same,
whether waiting for his dog to cross the creek,
or watched how trams on their glinty webs
ran spick spiders you might think them

as he thought back to the dog's shaking loose.
This man once set in the city so liked
to sit at an inexpensive café,
turn the squat glass which is coffee

and something else, just 'The special'
he knew to ask for. Men at other tables
spoke in the various ways men from other
places speak at such tables, happily,

disconsolately, while those who drink
alone, as he does, turn a glass
in their fingers, open their hands
to stroke the table they sit at,

move their palms across their faces,
the men with their bus fare should they care
to use it, the men who unlike the talkative
others need only their sparse phrases,

in the way so much as a single word
may cover a town let alone a province,
and whatever happens there you might think of,
the kitchens, the altars, the football

pools, the woman silent before her courage
allows her to speak. 'A Good Place'
the café is called in dialects of so many
kinds, 'A Good Place' looking the same

twenty years from now, the same
bright spiders where the rails curve.
A child with the name of a flower, the dog
breaking the stream, to think of as you wait.

Thinking the shark tank

The man who had no ambition to speak of,
a 'representative of the human condition' –
wasn't that enough? – liked to watch the shark
in the aquarium three inches of glass from
his own quiet smile, liked to imagine,
this normal and not especially lonely middle
aged man, if ever he thought of himself
as a writer, he'd go into the head of the shark,
he knew he'd be comfortable there, why not,
as nothing there would upset him,
nothing disturb; a man in the simple head
of a shark taking in such different people,
a child's hand pudging stars
on the glass, women whose lucubrations
he may never quite fathom, but here we are.
He knew, the man-shark, the shark-man, fairly
much what there was to know by looking out
at those who looked in with a tributary love.
You made allowance for so much. It took
all sorts. So much you'd know that would not
distress you, not having to find words for.

Note now you're back

You've been away a fortnight
and I've done as instructed down to
the last tomato picked this afternoon
the basil attended
the two hedgehogs fed that butt each other
to prove how close.

And entirely off my own bat
I've swept the cobwebs from the garage door
and the fence to the front steps
and this minute I've set this big glass
advertising *Orval* beer
                              on the TV table
so if one of the spiders who must loathe
me comes in to learn us, he's under the bell
of glass before you've time to shriek.

When I slip an envelope
between the glass and the spider
and return him, which is all he wants,
to his world of fractured highways,
and the business of lost cities to be restored.

Ah, the excellence of spiders!

Fieldwork

You do not tell by looking at a map
however precise, whether this is a map
of a real place or a made-up place or just *like* a map.

No one has ever sprained an ankle in a rabbit hole on a map.

Class outing, even now

When in Fourth Form it must have been, attending
a performance for the first time and no getting
out of, a Shakespeare company much of it over
her head, when that phrase 'a wilderness of monkeys'

so caught her, it was language's greeny net flung
over entire jungles, it was chitter in a million
branches, leapings at livid skies,
it was missing the next however many lines

she didn't take in, and for all the clever talk
in class on the Monday and the things you learned
about 'usury' exactly and for the first time
the word 'semitic', and Wendy Beckett's

arm waved off just about with the answers,
it was endless jibbering creatures held her eye.

Depression Villa

The house on the hill closed up at the end of summer.
The first of the last leaves claw at the veranda.
A man comes by once a week to check for mail.
The few times I have seen him leave his hands are empty.
'Shutters', a word there's no need for, yet it's said.
'Put up the shutters,' like that, of the shutterless house.
At the windows only a stranger looking in.

The house is above a beach with a derelict jetty.
A dog called Benjamin most days runs the sand.
A retriever that silks the wind, a russet scarf
It is always alone on the beach, exciting the surf.
The folk from the house are talked of but never seen.
The house is no more than the world when God moved off.
Empty as chairless kitchens as the wind pelts up.

How the bay there savagely rocks in the sudden wind.
How the house at sunset seems fired from within.
You watch as the flared west slaps against the glass.
By the time the stars are out, too late to invent.
Metaphor founders its dinghies in southerly swells.
You think last thing of the house, the shutterless house.
Its steeping tomorrow's absence before we wake.

Don't scrap though second-best

It was a boring I can tell you so boring
a room until you chanced in,
there was a curtain one wouldn't trust
to keep rain from a spider,
there were three vases dotted
around the room
                        each less lovely
than the one before or after whichever
you began from.

The bed made even 'rickety' seem an adjective
privileged in from Versailles.

And with us on the bed, *chérie*,
Lucien Freud may have considered
'At last, it's beyond me,'
fixing flesh as it is
to the occasion's aura.

It was as any lover insists
a journey from here to special places
then back to the vases, the curtain,
the plethora of *etceteras*.

Then dead honest announces, *'Mon amour*,
when lyric notches the ceiling
across the chosen shoulder,
you'll be first to know.'

At the city pound

I'm in charge of a cage. I know those that won't.
I don't mean can't. Just *won't*. There's a roster
for Tuesdays, Fridays. Dogs to die.

The disconsolate, the abandoned, those with recurrent
symptoms, the incorrigible mutt – oh, a dozen
choices by way of reasons. Even so,

some *won't*. Won't play along once their number's
up, the 'rainbow bridge' in the offing
as the posher clinics put it, a pig's ear

as a final treat, a venison chew, the profession
behaving beautifully at a time like this.
Still, those that won't. Won't go nicely, I mean,

with a gaze to melt, a last slobbed lick.
Those with a soul's defiance, though embarrassment
in the lunchroom should you come at that one.

Even after the bag is zipped, you feel it:
We're real at the end as you are, buster. We sniff
the wind. What say if we say it together? Won't.

On the table inside the window

a white old-fashioned doily
under a black vase

which could be what reality
would look like

were reality itself a negative
of how things are

so it's a white vase before
the photograph's developed

and the round doily
the surrounding shadow of the vase.

I am telling you this
because you may not have seen it,

the black light, its white shadow.

Unsuitable for children without supervision

The giant strides as he must through a giant's domain.
He would fondle the tiny creatures who applaud him,
pick and crush vertebrae, placing them kindly
in capacious pockets. He would sing them
the vast chastity of the sky as he follows its arc,
but his voice alone, a punishment, buckles them
to their knees. The stars *phut* to his salvos,
as if huffed-out matches. The giant deplores
how the modest streets run to rivers of fear.
'Make of me what you will then,' he is happy
to tell them. The billioned faces like tilted saucers
crack at the very notion, the children
who sit in his orchard as in the beautiful story
watch how his heartbreak lurches, tries
to redeem the so many blooms he fractures
en route. For what can they do but hate him,
his numberless children? The great Lord of Regrets,
as they secretly call him. His crushing concern.

Hers, then

See trees behind her in a swathe of photos.
Alphabet-trees the Celts could read by,
kahikatea at light's fading picnic,
olive branches turning as the wind switches.
In several the willows' yellowing arc,
the great swing of the Clutha's scything
current.
          So one might go on. Cypresses
spilling ink across Greek afternoons,
a kōwhai's dousing flare as it fumbles
towards dark. A Japanese maple in
a lacquered pot on a cool veranda.
Trees always on hand, as if tracking her
down.
          Yet an image I'd give the rest
for: mid-midsummer. The Kakanuis
hoarding blue in their rucked pleats,
their foreground the tilt as if something
molten, scoured: her head
caught in its turning, taking in all that.
All that as if for the century nothing
else intends. The treeless kingdom,
hers.

Well so I've heard

The man who fancied he was Xmas
died of a seizure
in the throes of illicit pleasure –
I'm not one to judge
but when he wouldn't budge
and must have weighed a ton
I thought, that's no way to spend Xmas.
He was lifted by crane
and the medics came
to attend his friend who lay thin as a curtain.
It would take a full year
to restore her *savoir faire*.
At least that much is certain.
Other details marked *Private* in the magistrate's folder.
Next Xmas is predicted to be colder.
Whiter. Pray God, much lighter.

Late Night News

'Vandals have slaughtered a colony of gulls.'
He or she walks among us, the barrel
still warm in the boot of a car.
We call in the clichés. 'What sort of . . .',
'Depraved, they must be', 'I know what
I'd do, the fuckers'. I know, too.
The he or she who squinted along
their sights, felt the trigger exult,
the blast of pure fun, pellets skittering
the inlet, I'd like them smiling, forever:
'We are the ones who killed the black-billed gulls.'

Poem with five plots

Père Lachaise:
My friend who pronounced it 'Pwoust' calls
out that he's found him. Black marble.
Gold lettering. Chrysanthemums lit
that morning. Sky. Trees. The city.
The endless lapse to the living past.

Oxford, Miss:
A cemetery so ordinary you know
how perfect. 'Beloved' on the headstone.
Autumn sifts and drifts. The man who shows
you says something like 'Missa Wim'.
The smell, whether there or not, of horses.
Closer still, verbena.

Sligo:
Again, whether here or not, mere bodily chatter.
Driving through veiling rain towards the west,
a tough squat church, the darkening trees
to either side. Too easy to say, 'a hawk'.
The famous stone where the sentence lies.

Vienna:
One I'd like to have been at. A few
men. A tearless woman. The odd spy,
who else? I think I've seen photos of it.
So hard to remember. Was the great Wheel
in sight from the graveside? The *Allees* seemed
so much longer. A match strikes on the way out.

A choice of several places:
More likely these days a parcel a relative cradles.
Or several take turns to pass like a halfback
out to the wings. A mordant image.
If the wind's right, dust between the posts.

Some time back, I saw it

A video of women about to die in China.
Their hair washed and combed the night before,
the modest pile of clothes they leave for friends.
Women who knew the privilege of minutes, of living
sons, of dying with shining hair, unlatching
lockets from their throats. Last things done well.

Rides by arrangement only

There are few things I puzzle at more than theologians not accepting
        'elephant' as a codeword, as it seems to me,
        for magnificent absence.

I imagine a roomful of atheists denying the elephant in the room,
        as they fiddle the trinkets of history
        slivered into yellow toothpicks.

I admire to the point of hero-worship that man in a French novel
        who first apprehended how civilisation
        rides the backs of such creatures.

'The end of elephants – concede it – would be the end of us.'
        After the trumpeting, the deluge. The last
        trunked question mark against

livid skies. One waits to see it, the final devotional
        object being an elephant's foot,
        the names of the twelve tribes,

the minute inscribing of gospels, mantra, a choice Bach
        cantata, on the half-circles of its nails,
        arcades of arcana.

As a burial fantasy: the raking blare of a herd's
        final obbligato, our souls timid, our minds
        numbed. It must be a symbol

for so much. For the last trunks' entwining, the wet
        toothless droop of regret.
        For the buckling knees.

Well, the point of names

Small blue flowers with a flash of white spill over
their pot, near a black fence, call out for attention.
'Just flowers,' you can say, 'they're nice there, aren't they?'
Or lobelia, and the patch burns with what it is.

Know what a thing's called, and we own it; if not,
there's really only pointing, our still wishing
we knew. The afternoon wilts round its edges,
unless we've *said* it. A name is like wearing

a watch that tells you, all is here on time.
A big dog, a child says, a nasty man on TV.
'Sure,' we say. But tell us, 'Baxter from the dairy',
or, 'The man dad likes to call Simple Simon',

and we're in this together. We're holding
hands. 'Let's go into the garden and give it
names.' This is before it rains. Or gets too
mushy. The whole place waiting to take home.

Woodsman

Apart from in nursery rhymes, Russian
poetry, movies, I doubt I've seen one.
A woodsman. His axe that can bring down
birches, or at lunchtime, pare cheese.

The word has something kindly about it,
though trees must hate it. 'Don't even finish
the word!' a larch shivers, and the orchard, maybe,
shaking enough to bring apples down.

Yet nothing a woodsman likes more than to loll
in summer, eye a tree too perfect to consider.
The trouble being, he admits, counting notches
on his handle, how do you know unless it falls?

A story from the Forties

I used to wet my hair at the backyard tap
and comb a slab flat on my forehead,
then put a finger inside the chimney
for a soot moustache. Hitler wasn't dead.

I'd strut about in my khaki shirt,
Donald from next door would go
goofy with his front teeth, squint
behind his glasses. He was Tojo.

No one, as I remember, ever
wanted to be Stalin, though Rusty Smith
had him on the wall in their kitchen,
the way we had Mr Savage. A girl with

a thick boot but a bosom and very
pretty, further down the street, let
us see her lie on her bed with a blue cloak
and a white veil. She was St Bernadette.

I stood on a box and raised my arm,
Tojo gabbled Japanese. He painted a red
circle on the side of his trolley.
'Don't you dare!' someone shouted when I said

it would be a joke to scare the family
in the white house who had got away, just.
Donald's old man had enough of this caper.
'Try to be bloody normal!' Teresa's father must

have given the same advice. She wouldn't
be dead and holy and let us touch
her titties politely as people do with saints,
to fix gammy legs and blind eyes and oh, so much.

So there we were, back to boring normal.
Donald became a pilot. Teresa married rich.
I taught a thousand kids over forty years,
'Try not to be foxed by history, the bitch.'

Delight

To watch a granddaughter rowing on a lake.
Too early to see the eucalypts clearly, but they charge the air.

The clip far off, and then near, the oars
with their fringe of white, the sky paling to the beat.

The boat sleeks level, then past, thin as a pencil.
A pencil writing the lake's slate page.

Although not meant to say so

When Dr S. taught us Philosophy One
we liked to think her mind cut a figure.
We frothed at the way she said 'Kant' like a German.
We couldn't wait for her next sentence.
At times she'd take ages just to take off
one word. At others, in a flurry,
as with brides descending a staircase,
an argument sashayed across the room
and out, into radiant truth. Even,
as a rather sad colleague put it, a syllogism
can break a bra strap, a proposition
smuggle across borders like a hidden
canary. We adored her, even in exams.

South, because we had to

So long ago who's to prove if I'm wrong.
About the mountain, the great snows crafted
against a serious moon. Everything in the night
so empty that wasn't us, and the rocking train.

I didn't think at the time and could not have
how the moon slides over the big harbour
we'll be at by morning, across the wood
on the top of where she's lying, and the sun

not tomorrow but after tomorrow
when the uncles tilt her a little on the way
out to the long car that is Wellington black,
the sun out like for special and down, down.

The big hooty tunnel I always wait for.
My uncle's dog called Kerry
that leans from the car window
and dies of earache a long time later.

Across the road from the house straight onto
the beach. Waves that stand green caves
for their halted second, then break,
glass curving until it cracks.

But the mountain and the moon,
That's what a boy remembers. Wants to
remember. Not everything else.
Everything walking slowly behind the wood.

Blanket Bay

At the inlet where 'foundering fathers'
drowned with their children however many
tides back,
      half a dozen white spoonbills
take in the afternoon, a pair of black
shags share the half-drowned branches,
weird keys the breeze plays at.

There is no moral to be drawn. The facts
speak hushly enough few halfway hear
them.
      The spoonbills. The shags.
The drenched Scottish children sleeping.
Another day being another day, wherever
it occurs. The promise the white keys
bring. The sadness, the black.

Even now, in winter

Even now, in winter,
    it is raining in Greenland, the rain
    softly nails at the eaves of the Pole,
    brings the roof down with it: the white
    bears on their drifting verandas,
    a paw print no longer a print, a miniature
    lake.
        Even now, in winter.
                Now, even
in summer. Tides climb on the rocks,
    the rocks founder, sodden: bones white
    as scraps of leftover winters
    signed on as something new, orcas
    on what was mid-channel, now churning
    mud.
        Even now, in summer.
               Summer
and winter stretching towards each other
    as brother autumn, sister spring, shrink
    to leaner names.
        A man measures
the no longer there to be measured, the too
    much by far immeasurable sea.
The wind hauls at different sledges.
Even now in winter,
        summer,
        in winter's summer.

Frogheart
for Herbert

I don't remember how long it is since I last heard
frogs. I didn't enjoy it, as a child, tagging along
with bigger kids, carrying back one of the fat
jam jars with its slimed water, tadpoles
you nearly saw through, and mothers said,
'The excellence of watching nature work,'
as if the jar I lugged was something special.

Most plumped and died and floated on their sides,
slivered bloated glass, their bulgy heads,
poured out onto a pile of backyard grass.
First pictures I saw of human embryos
I thought, hang on, I've seen this lot before.
So much falls into place once that's on board.
'Nature at work', but don't pretend it's *nice*.

The few that made it through, grand ugly
fun. The brilliant green, the pump as if all else
except their legs was frogheart, the splay of toes
toy dinosaurs, their nervy leap
to nowhere, but *away*, into the sound they came
for – ripping brocades to shreds, then ripped again.

As Sinclaire promised in Standard Six

You'll love the rodeo, promise, it's like a shock
belts through the arcing horse from mouth to cock,
makes it mad as shit. It flings and rears,
kicks in the rider's head for all it cares.
Sometimes they carry the tossed up jokers off
on stretchers. 'Christ,' he says, 'you'd laugh
your arse off. Never though seen one dead.'
It turned out even better than he said.
Some Aussie outback cowboy flung so high
you'd think a hook had yanked him to the sky,
then dropped him, gollywogged, across the rails.
(Never a day but someone *really* fails.)
The horse's leg bone sticking so far out
three men hold up a canvas while it's shot.
Not a real bullet mind. Just *thud*.
After the first rodeo, most turn out dud.

A binding agreement with reality

that whatever occurs, or does not occur,
accidents, intentions, delights, trauma writ large,
including divagations from imagined counsel,
no complaints may legally be entered into,
divergent versions offered for media release,
written up as memo, memoir, *memento
mori*, fate: neither 'ought' nor 'somewhat'
accepted, *contra* written consent.
Nothing (as appears in fine print, next
item) in the non-signator's background regarding
day and night, extremities and habits,
bear consequence on terms as generally applied.
A signature is not essential whatever one's creed,
hapū, proclivities, or medical state.
Your acceptance confirms no undeclared agenda.
You may now proceed to be born.

The thinker in the greenhouse

Philosophy has so helped me over the years.
The kind where the words fight the things the things
insist they are. There is little I am not receptive
to, once 'receptive' is defined. How
can one not accept the demand to be exact?

I change flowerpots about in the small conservatory
my wife speaks of as though Kew isn't in the running.
She tells me the pretty speckled yellow pillows
are calceolaria. She advises never to question
the Latin of those with green fingers, the quality
of garlic depends on its grower speaking French.
In the light of the conservatory we seem to touch
more often. We are less likely to regret.

As though a boy, my popping the fuchsia buds
to a little war of their own. True gardeners
deplore, quite rightly, this inventing allegory
as fun. Nature *intends*. There are limits to pleasure.

My wife instructs, too, certain plants that sting
one has no right to speak of unless one has been stung.
In late afternoon, there is something cloistered to a greenhouse.
There is the faintest chanting one all but hears.
Something is winging through. You are part of the wing.

Dogspeed

Dogspeed, are you ready? The always road?
The dog with three legs is ready.
The dog with the ribs you can count,
nosing the gutters. The outcast even
among dogs, that follows the dead,
its tongue sweet still from licking.

So often there, have you noticed that,
when News resurrects, as the announcer tells you,
'Shooting has been constant,' or, 'The suicide
bomber unidentified, but presumed . . .'

The same woman who is cast to go
from one corpse to another, her head scarfed,
hands raw with age, with tending
the bodies she is desperate still to tend . . .

And the dogs go with her. A long shot
of a jagged street its locals left
at midnight. See the lean dog
tamp at steaming brick. It makes
what it can of a town so suddenly flat.

Do they travel together, one slaughter
to another? Glad of each other's
company, a rough kind of comfort?
The mother with her veils, her agitated
hands, the dog knowing its distance,
the cur, the mutt, the hound, the outcast,
as if in some way it attends her,
the inconsolable traveller. Its eyes quick
as a sniper's. Its chance will come.

There is no sentiment with dogs. No one
leaves a note hoping a dog may read it.
No one tells them the code. A dog
dies where it must, as though timed
exactly. The *requiescat* they're spared.

'Dogspeed' we may imagine calling
at the end of a clip, knowing we'll spot
it tomorrow on tomorrow's News.
While the TV's off, it travels. All the time it's got.

Travel for the young

The absent girl so constantly present
in her plaster mould, *all the way
from Pompeii*, says a girl in Texas,
in Wellington, Macao. 'I wish we could
touch her,' which museums don't allow.

'Unlimited travel', a frank deity might
have put it beforehand, when the first
pebbles troubled the terracotta
tiles, asking 'Ready to go?'
at the darker than usual opening door.

Politics at the patisserie

It was nice of Marie Antoinette to say what she did.
A head of her time. How her words have rung!
A cake is worth a vote in any tongue.
Two cakes being sufficient to buy off a vote.
(Three cakes, one promises never again to vote.)

A candied podium may equal a throne.
A four sponge general runs a state alone.
Let them. Let them. Let them.
Then forget them, the words she said.
For a lovely lady's sake we still shout for bread.

A poem rightly not much cared for

It is not essential but helps to be middle class
to write poems about how lovely people holiday
in places where the average monthly income
would cover less than half a new bikini.

Poems of that nature are often sincere,
the way Franco Zeffirelli, say, was sincere
depicting a very poor couple in a production
too expensive finally to be staged.

When you are home again for a month or so
after the marvellous sunsets and the plaintive
hymns at a funeral across from the resort
you were invited to attend, almost too sensitive

to think of intruding, you look at the images
there in high-res detail and colour, wonder
what's so leached from memory, in so little
time? The word *astonishing* sounds the same

but not the intensity, does that make sense?
Astonishing, mating up, again, and none of it
planned! But a word too is a wave and timing
is all, you might say, in catching it early,

riding it correctly, which means as it rightly
demands. This is a love poem after its fashion.
It is put discreetly, a passion that prefers
to rollick in private. A shade let down.

To be mocked, at peril

In a Melbourne paper, forty years back:
'Woman with mild cleft palate
hopes to meet hairy sheep-shearer.'

I know the pressures of PC
that shackle frankness of certain
kinds, but heavenly Jesus,

one can't but love them, the children
of such candour, the bravery
to say, 'Think what you like, you

urban wankers, I know what I'm after.'
We have, as we read, our fantasies.
Mine is to see them in the outback,

the nights for their sake longer and longer,
the first dawning of the gums to instant
sweetness, the crackle of birds.

When they're more than a mile apart,
they start thinking, *home*.
Two miles or three, love's panic.

Playback, if only

I talk with a girl I was crazy enough
about to take tennis lessons for and make
her reasons for not feeling the same, complete.

She smiles in a way that makes sixty years
seem a turn or two around the block,
as her mind shuffles the cards wrongly.

'Life isn't all bad,' she jokes. 'I can still
taste Cointreau!' But goes to the wrong
bottle as she pours it. I wait for sixty

seconds hoping I've got it wrong – the quirky
tilt of elaborate mirrors, the *wayang* puppets,
the curtains half drawn against the view.

I would like to go through the cards with her,
to rearrange correctly the dominant facts,
how they were, are meant to be. A year

for each year would be long enough to do it.
Rage for its hot moment smothers
my eyes. I take the glass with the wrong

liqueur, we tap the delicate rims.
Eye to eye, we toast how things ought to be.
The lie that perfects the lie of time as it is.

Lines for a book launch

A killjoy of sorts may tell you how celebrity
is a have, as they say, not being irreducibly
final: another stripper may prance in the wings
whose instant force erases previous glitter

by finer skills, wry parody, sheer inventive
twitch. Oh how history wheels, a star melts
completely, another already, *twinkliest
little star*. Such being heaven's way.

The girl in the spotlit moment gives the arse,
as they also say, to the solemn thinker,
his face prolonged as Tennyson's thinking of *Maud*.

Get with it, Alf! Glasses beat
on the bar, lights flare, fresh quivery cheeks
scoop instant fame: poetry twerking prose.

Southern pastoral

When you see a Merc or a Lexus pulling
up at a farm gate and a man in slacks
and a lady in high heels steps carefully
as the man holds out his hand to assist
her, you know you're on the verge
of the pastoral as an art form.
You want to call a composer friend
to have soft horns in the background
and a saxophone, yes, a saxophone
tracing a line of McCahon-like hills,
because they have a McCahon too,
and a wallfull of patient disconsolate birds.
That's what Corin has, what Phoebe
has, what they will equally share
should it ever, which pray it won't come to,
on lawyers' advice . . .
                                        The agent reminds,
'Watch where you're stepping, Phoebe,'
and Corin's hand-sewn Italian boot
prodding the rung of the gate as he'd seen
on *Country Calendar* time and again.
Phoebe takes Corin's hand, he hers.
They look to the perfectly doctored slope
down to the lake, the wee perfect beach.
The snow on the peaks across the lake
which, the agent jokes, comes free
with the view. We'll take it, Corin nods.
A pity the snow's not ours though, Phoebe.

Since you kindly enquire, in the elevator, yes

I've had a good life. Cosy, mildly frayed here
and there at the edges of the canvas,
much of it undeservedly beneath the peace dove's
wing, safer than had I learned to drive,
or mended steeples, loitered at home and painted
as genuine artists do, or breathed down
phones, given the example of others more
into doppelgängers.
                              The grand thing
about *words* is few expect, as they once did,
the gilded truth. Poets now find it harder
to put across offensive verses, this being
not so much a testament as answering
what you asked on the *pied-à-terre*,
and now with slowing as we get to the flash
disclosures of the penthouse, must
inevitably be answered: Fine, thank
you. Great. And you? Things OK with you?